John
Tells the Good News

A quick look at this book

In the beginning – page 1

Jesus the Light of the world – page 27

The death of Lazarus – page 36

Jesus the way to the Father – page 48

Jesus sentenced to death – page 61

Death defeated – page 64

Footnotes – page 70

This edition of the Gospel of John is taken from the *Holy Bible*, New Living Translation, British text, copyright © 2000, an anglicised version of the *Holy Bible*, New Living Translation.

Holy Bible, New Living Translation, copyright © 1996, by Tyndale Charitable Trust. All rights reserved.

Cover Design by ICP copyright © 2004

The text of the *Holy Bible*, New Living Translation, may be quoted in any form (written, visual, electronic, or audio) up to and inclusive of two hundred and fifty (250) verses without express written permission of the publisher, provided that the verses quoted do not account for more than 20% of the work in which they are quoted, and provided that a complete book of the Bible is not quoted. When the *Holy Bible*, New Living Translation, is quoted, the following credit lines must appear on the copyright page or title page of the work:

Scripture quotations marked (NLT) are taken from the *Holy Bible*, New Living Translation, copyright © 1996. Used by permission of Tyndale House Publishers, Inc, Wheaton, Illinois 60189. All rights reserved.

When quotations from the NLT are used in nonsaleable media, such as church bulletins, orders of service, newsletters, transparencies, or similar media, a complete copyright notice is not required, but the initials (NLT) must appear at the end of each quotation.

Quotations in excess of two hundred and fifty (250) verses or 20% of the work, or other permission requests, must be directed to and approved in writing by Tyndale House Publishers, Inc. P.O. Box 80, Wheaton, Illinois 60189, USA.

New Living, NLT, and the New Living Translation logo are trademarks of Tyndale House Publishers, Inc.

ISBN 0 – 9015.1849 – 2   2005/20M

Published by: The Scottish Bible Society, 7 Hampton Terrace, Edinburgh, EH12 5XU

Typesetting copyright © The Scottish Bible Society.

Typeset in Souvenir BQ by Solidus www.solid-us.com

Printed in Italy by Lego s.p.a.

CHAPTER 1

Christ, the Eternal Word

In the beginning the Word already existed. He was with God, and he was God. ²He was in the beginning with God. ³He created everything there is. Nothing exists that he didn't make. ⁴Life itself was in him, and this life gives light to everyone. ⁵The light shines through the darkness, and the darkness can never extinguish it.

⁶God sent John the Baptist ⁷to tell everyone about the light so that everyone might believe because of his testimony. ⁸John himself was not the light; he was only a witness to the light. ⁹The one who is the true light, who gives light to everyone, was going to come into the world.

¹⁰But although the world was made through him, the world didn't recognize him when he came. ¹¹Even in his own land and among his own people, he was not accepted. ¹²But to all who believed him and accepted him, he gave the right to become children of God. ¹³They are reborn! This is not a physical birth resulting from human passion or plan—this rebirth comes from God.

¹⁴So the Word became human and lived here on earth among us. He was full of unfailing love and faithfulness.* And we have seen his glory, the glory of the only Son of the Father.

¹⁵John pointed him out to the people. He shouted to the crowds, "This is the one I was talking about when I said, 'Someone is coming who is far greater than I am, for he existed long before I did.'"

¹⁶We have all benefited from the rich blessings he brought to us—one gracious blessing after another.*

[17] For the law was given through Moses; God's unfailing love and faithfulness came through Jesus Christ. [18] No one has ever seen God. But his only Son, who is himself God,* is near to the Father's heart; he has told us about him.

The Testimony of John the Baptist

[19] This was the testimony of John when the Jewish leaders sent priests and Temple assistants* from Jerusalem to ask John whether he claimed to be the Messiah. [20] He flatly denied it. "I am not the Messiah," he said.

[21] "Well then, who are you?" they asked. "Are you Elijah?"

"No," he replied.

"Are you the Prophet?"*

"No."

[22] "Then who are you? Tell us, so we can give an answer to those who sent us. What do you have to say about yourself?"

[23] John replied in the words of Isaiah:

"I am a voice shouting in the wilderness,

'Prepare a straight pathway for the Lord's coming!' "*
[24] Then those who were sent by the Pharisees [25] asked him, "If you aren't the Messiah or Elijah or the Prophet, what right do you have to baptize?"

[26] John told them, "I baptize with* water, but right here in the crowd is someone you do not know, [27] who will soon begin his ministry. I am not even worthy to be his slave.*" [28] This incident took place at Bethany, a village east of the River Jordan, where John was baptizing.

Jesus, the Lamb of God

29 The next day John saw Jesus coming towards him and said, "Look! There is the Lamb of God who takes away the sin of the world! 30 He is the one I was talking about when I said, 'Soon a man is coming who is far greater than I am, for he existed long before I did.' 31 I didn't know he was the one, but I have been baptizing with water in order to point him out to Israel."

32 Then John said, "I saw the Holy Spirit descending like a dove from heaven and resting upon him. 33 I didn't know he was the one, but when God sent me to baptize with water, he told me, 'When you see the Holy Spirit descending and resting upon someone, he is the one you are looking for. He is the one who baptizes with the Holy Spirit.' 34 I saw this happen to Jesus, so I testify that he is the Son of God.*"

The First Disciples

35 The following day, John was again standing with two of his disciples. 36 As Jesus walked by, John looked at him and then declared, "Look! There is the Lamb of God!" 37 Then John's two disciples turned and followed Jesus.

38 Jesus looked around and saw them following. "What do you want?" he asked them.

They replied, "Rabbi" (which means Teacher), "where are you staying?"

39 "Come and see," he said. It was about four o'clock in the afternoon when they went with him to the place, and they stayed there the rest of the day.

40 Andrew, Simon Peter's brother, was one of these men who had heard what John said and then followed Jesus.

⁴¹ The first thing Andrew did was to find his brother, Simon, and tell him, "We have found the Messiah" (which means the Christ).

⁴² Then Andrew brought Simon to meet Jesus. Looking intently at Simon, Jesus said, "You are Simon, the son of John—but you will be called Cephas" (which means Peter*).

⁴³ The next day Jesus decided to go to Galilee. He found Philip and said to him, "Come, be my disciple." ⁴⁴ Philip was from Bethsaida, Andrew and Peter's home town.

⁴⁵ Philip went off to look for Nathanael and told him, "We have found the very person Moses and the prophets wrote about! His name is Jesus, the son of Joseph from Nazareth."

⁴⁶ "Nazareth!" exclaimed Nathanael. "Can anything good come from there?"

"Just come and see for yourself," Philip said.

⁴⁷ As they approached, Jesus said, "Here comes an honest man—a true son of Israel."

⁴⁸ "How do you know about me?" Nathanael asked.

And Jesus replied, "I could see you under the fig tree before Philip found you."

⁴⁹ Nathanael replied, "Teacher, you are the Son of God—the King of Israel!"

⁵⁰ Jesus asked him, "Do you believe all this just because I told you I had seen you under the fig tree? You will see greater things than this." ⁵¹ Then he said, "The truth is, you will all see heaven open and the angels of God going up and down upon the Son of Man."*

CHAPTER 2

The Wedding at Cana

The next day* Jesus' mother was a guest at a wedding celebration in the village of Cana in Galilee. ²Jesus and his disciples were also invited to the celebration. ³The wine supply ran out during the festivities, so Jesus' mother spoke to him about the problem. "They have no more wine," she told him.

⁴"How does that concern you and me?" Jesus asked. "My time has not yet come."

⁵But his mother told the servants, "Do whatever he tells you."

⁶Six stone waterpots were standing there; they were used for Jewish ceremonial purposes and held seventy-five to a hundred litres* each. ⁷Jesus told the servants, "Fill the jars with water." When the jars had been filled to the brim, ⁸he said, "Draw some out and take it to the master of ceremonies." So they followed his instructions.

⁹When the master of ceremonies tasted the water that was now wine, not knowing where it had come from (though, of course, the servants knew), he called the bridegroom over. ¹⁰"Usually a host serves the best wine first," he said. "Then, when everyone is full and doesn't care, he brings out the less expensive wines. But you have kept the best until now!"

¹¹This miraculous sign at Cana in Galilee was Jesus' first display of his glory. And his disciples believed in him.

¹²After the wedding he went to Capernaum for a few days with his mother, his brothers, and his disciples.

Jesus Clears the Temple

¹³ It was time for the annual Passover celebration, and Jesus went to Jerusalem. ¹⁴ In the Temple area he saw merchants selling cattle, sheep, and doves for sacrifices; and he saw money changers behind their counters. ¹⁵ Jesus made a whip from some ropes and chased them all out of the Temple. He drove out the sheep and oxen, scattered the money changers' coins over the floor, and turned over their tables. ¹⁶ Then, going over to the people who sold doves, he told them, "Get these things out of here. Don't turn my Father's house into a marketplace!"

¹⁷ Then his disciples remembered this prophecy from the Scriptures: "Passion for God's house burns within me."*

¹⁸ "What right do you have to do these things?" the Jewish leaders demanded. "If you have this authority from God, show us a miraculous sign to prove it."

¹⁹ "All right," Jesus replied. "Destroy this temple, and in three days I will raise it up."

²⁰ "What!" they exclaimed. "It took forty-six years to build this Temple, and you can do it in three days?" ²¹ But by "this temple," Jesus meant his body. ²² After he was raised from the dead, the disciples remembered that he had said this. And they believed both Jesus and the Scriptures.

²³ Because of the miraculous signs he did in Jerusalem at the Passover celebration, many people were convinced that he was indeed the Messiah. ²⁴ But Jesus didn't trust them, because he knew what people were really like. ²⁵ No one needed to tell him about human nature.

CHAPTER 3

Jesus and Nicodemus

After dark one evening, a Jewish religious leader named Nicodemus, a Pharisee, ²came to speak with Jesus. "Teacher," he said, "we all know that God has sent you to teach us. Your miraculous signs are proof enough that God is with you."

³Jesus replied, "I assure you, unless you are born again,* you can never see the Kingdom of God."

⁴"What do you mean?" exclaimed Nicodemus. "How can an old man go back into his mother's womb and be born again?"

⁵Jesus replied, "The truth is, no one can enter the Kingdom of God without being born of water and the Spirit.* ⁶Humans can reproduce only human life, but the Holy Spirit gives new life from heaven. ⁷So don't be surprised at my statement that you* must be born again. ⁸Just as you can hear the wind but can't tell where it comes from or where it is going, so you can't explain how people are born of the Spirit."

⁹"What do you mean?" Nicodemus asked.

¹⁰Jesus replied, "You are a respected Jewish teacher, and yet you don't understand these things? ¹¹I assure you, I am telling you what we know and have seen, and yet you won't believe us. ¹²But if you don't even believe me when I tell you about things that happen here on earth, how can you possibly believe if I tell you what is going on in heaven? ¹³For only I, the Son of Man,* have come to earth and will return to heaven again. ¹⁴And as Moses lifted up the bronze snake on a pole in the

wilderness, so I, the Son of Man, must be lifted up on a pole,* ¹⁵ so that everyone who believes in me will have eternal life.

¹⁶ "For God so loved the world that he gave his only Son, so that everyone who believes in him will not perish but have eternal life. ¹⁷ God did not send his Son into the world to condemn it, but to save it.

¹⁸ "There is no judgement awaiting those who trust him. But those who do not trust him have already been judged for not believing in the only Son of God. ¹⁹ Their judgement is based on this fact: The light from heaven came into the world, but they loved the darkness more than the light, for their actions were evil. ²⁰ They hate the light because they want to sin in the darkness. They stay away from the light for fear their sins will be exposed and they will be punished. ²¹ But those who do what is right come to the light gladly, so everyone can see that they are doing what God wants."

John the Baptist Exalts Jesus

²² Afterwards Jesus and his disciples left Jerusalem, but they stayed in Judea for a while and baptized there.

²³ At this time John the Baptist was baptizing at Aenon, near Salim, because there was plenty of water there and people kept coming to him for baptism. ²⁴ This was before John was put into prison. ²⁵ At that time a certain Jew began an argument with John's disciples over ceremonial cleansing. ²⁶ John's disciples came to him and said, "Teacher, the man you met on the other side of the River Jordan, the one you said was the Messiah, is also baptizing people. And everybody is going over there instead of coming here to us."

²⁷John replied, "God in heaven appoints each person's work. ²⁸You yourselves know how plainly I told you that I am not the Messiah. I am here to prepare the way for him—that is all. ²⁹The bride will go where the bridegroom is. A bridegroom's friend rejoices with him. I am the bridegroom's friend, and I am filled with joy at his success. ³⁰He must become greater and greater, and I must become less and less.

³¹"He has come from above and is greater than anyone else. I am of the earth, and my understanding is limited to the things of earth, but he has come from heaven.* ³²He tells what he has seen and heard, but how few believe what he tells them! ³³Those who believe him discover that God is true. ³⁴For he is sent by God. He speaks God's words, for God's Spirit is upon him without measure or limit. ³⁵The Father loves his Son, and he has given him authority over everything. ³⁶And all who believe in God's Son have eternal life. Those who don't obey the Son will never experience eternal life, but the wrath of God remains upon them."

CHAPTER 4

Jesus and the Samaritan Woman

Jesus* learned that the Pharisees had heard, "Jesus is baptizing and making more disciples than John" ²(though Jesus himself didn't baptize them—his disciples did). ³So he left Judea to return to Galilee.

⁴He had to go through Samaria on the way. ⁵Eventually he came to the Samaritan village of Sychar, near the parcel of ground that Jacob gave to his son Joseph.

⁶ Jacob's well was there; and Jesus, tired from the long walk, sat wearily beside the well about midday. ⁷ Soon a Samaritan woman came to draw water, and Jesus said to her, "Please give me a drink." ⁸ He was alone at the time because his disciples had gone into the village to buy some food.

⁹ The woman was surprised, for Jews refuse to have anything to do with Samaritans. She said to Jesus, "You are a Jew, and I am a Samaritan woman. Why are you asking me for a drink?"

¹⁰ Jesus replied, "If you only knew the gift God has for you and who I am, you would ask me, and I would give you living water."

¹¹ "But sir, you don't have a rope or a bucket," she said, "and this is a very deep well. Where would you get this living water? ¹² And besides, are you greater than our ancestor Jacob who gave us this well? How can you offer better water than he and his sons and his cattle enjoyed?"

¹³ Jesus replied, "People soon become thirsty again after drinking this water. ¹⁴ But the water I give them takes away thirst altogether. It becomes a perpetual spring within them, giving them eternal life."

¹⁵ "Please, sir," the woman said, "give me some of that water! Then I'll never be thirsty again, and I won't have to come here to haul water."

¹⁶ "Go and get your husband," Jesus told her.

¹⁷ "I don't have a husband," the woman replied.

Jesus said, "You're right! You don't have a husband—¹⁸ for you have had five husbands, and you aren't even married to the man you're living with now."

¹⁹ "Sir," the woman said, "you must be a prophet. ²⁰ So tell me, why is it that you Jews insist that Jerusalem is the only place of worship, while we Samaritans claim it is here at Mount Gerizim,* where our ancestors worshipped?"

²¹ Jesus replied, "Believe me, the time is coming when it will no longer matter whether you worship the Father here or in Jerusalem. ²² You Samaritans know so little about the one you worship, while we Jews know all about him, for salvation comes through the Jews. ²³ But the time is coming and is already here when true worshippers will worship the Father in spirit and in truth. The Father is looking for anyone who will worship him that way. ²⁴ For God is Spirit, so those who worship him must worship in spirit and in truth."

²⁵ The woman said, "I know the Messiah will come—the one who is called Christ. When he comes, he will explain everything to us."

²⁶ Then Jesus told her, "I am the Messiah!"*

²⁷ Just then his disciples arrived. They were astonished to find him talking to a woman, but none of them asked him why he was doing it or what they had been discussing. ²⁸ The woman left her water jar beside the well and went back to the village and told everyone, ²⁹ "Come and meet a man who told me everything I've ever done! Can this be the Messiah?" ³⁰ So the people came streaming from the village to see him.

³¹ Meanwhile, the disciples were urging Jesus to eat. ³² "No," he said, "I have food you don't know about."

³³ "Who brought it to him?" the disciples asked each other.

11

[34] Then Jesus explained: "My nourishment comes from doing the will of God, who sent me, and from finishing his work. [35] Do you think the work of harvesting will not begin until the summer ends four months from now? Look around you! Vast fields are ripening all around us and are ready now for the harvest. [36] The harvesters are paid good wages, and the fruit they harvest is people brought to eternal life. What joy awaits both the planter and the harvester alike! [37] You know the saying, 'One person plants and someone else harvests.' And it's true. [38] I sent you to harvest where you didn't plant; others had already done the work, and you will gather the harvest."

Many Samaritans Believe

[39] Many Samaritans from the village believed in Jesus because the woman had said, "He told me everything I've ever done!" [40] When they came out to see him, they begged him to stay at their village. So he stayed for two days, [41] long enough for many of them to hear his message and believe. [42] Then they said to the woman, "Now we believe because we have heard him ourselves, not just because of what you told us. He is indeed the Saviour of the world."

Jesus Heals an Official's Son

[43] At the end of the two days' stay, Jesus went on into Galilee. [44] He had previously said, "A prophet is honoured everywhere except in his own country." [45] The Galileans welcomed him, for they had been in Jerusalem at the Passover celebration and had seen all his miraculous signs.

[46] In the course of his journey through Galilee, he arrived at the town of Cana, where he had turned the

water into wine. There was a government official in the city of Capernaum whose son was very sick. ⁴⁷When he heard that Jesus had come from Judea and was travelling in Galilee, he went over to Cana. He found Jesus and begged him to come to Capernaum with him to heal his son, who was about to die.

⁴⁸Jesus asked, "Must I do miraculous signs and wonders before you people will believe in me?"

⁴⁹The official pleaded, "Lord, please come now before my little boy dies."

⁵⁰Then Jesus told him, "Go back home. Your son will live!" And the man believed Jesus' word and started home.

⁵¹While he was on his way, some of his servants met him with the news that his son was alive and well. ⁵²He asked them when the boy had begun to feel better, and they replied, "Yesterday afternoon at one o'clock his fever suddenly disappeared!" ⁵³Then the father realized it was the same time that Jesus had told him, "Your son will live." And the officer and his entire household believed in Jesus. ⁵⁴This was Jesus' second miraculous sign in Galilee after coming from Judea.

CHAPTER 5

Jesus Heals a Lame Man

Afterwards Jesus returned to Jerusalem for one of the Jewish holy days. ²Inside the city, near the Sheep Gate, was the pool of Bethesda,* with five covered porches. ³Crowds of sick people—blind, lame, or paralysed—lay on the porches.* ⁵One of the men lying there had been sick for thirty-eight years. [6] When Jesus saw him and knew how long he had been ill, he asked him, "Would you like to get well?"

[7] "I can't, sir," the sick man said, "for I have no one to help me into the pool when the water is stirred up. While I am trying to get there, someone else always gets in ahead of me."

[8] Jesus told him, "Stand up, pick up your sleeping mat, and walk!"

[9] Instantly, the man was healed! He rolled up the mat and began walking! But this miracle happened on the Sabbath day. [10] So the Jewish leaders objected. They said to the man who was cured, "You can't work on the Sabbath! It's illegal to carry that sleeping mat!"

[11] He replied, "The man who healed me said to me, 'Pick up your sleeping mat and walk.' "

[12] "Who said such a thing as that?" they demanded.

[13] The man didn't know, for Jesus had disappeared into the crowd. [14] But afterwards Jesus found him in the Temple and told him, "Now you are well; so stop sinning, or something even worse may happen to you." [15] Then the man went to find the Jewish leaders and told them it was Jesus who had healed him.

Jesus Claims to Be the Son of God

[16] So the Jewish leaders began harassing Jesus for breaking the Sabbath rules. [17] But Jesus replied, "My Father never stops working, so why should I?" [18] So the Jewish leaders tried all the more to kill him. In addition to disobeying the Sabbath rules, he had spoken of God as his Father, thereby making himself equal with God.

¹⁹ Jesus replied, "I assure you, the Son can do nothing by himself. He does only what he sees the Father doing. Whatever the Father does, the Son also does. ²⁰ For the Father loves the Son and tells him everything he is doing, and the Son will do far greater things than healing this man. You will be astonished at what he does. ²¹ He will even raise from the dead anyone he wants to, just as the Father does. ²² And the Father leaves all judgement to his Son, ²³ so that everyone will honour the Son, just as they honour the Father. But if you refuse to honour the Son, then you are certainly not honouring the Father who sent him.

²⁴ "I assure you, those who listen to my message and believe in God who sent me have eternal life. They will never be condemned for their sins, but they have already passed from death into life.

²⁵ "And I assure you that the time is coming, in fact it is here, when the dead will hear my voice—the voice of the Son of God. And those who listen will live. ²⁶ The Father has life in himself, and he has granted his Son to have life in himself. ²⁷ And he has given him authority to judge all mankind because he is the Son of Man. ²⁸ Don't be so surprised! Indeed, the time is coming when all the dead in their graves will hear the voice of God's Son, ²⁹ and they will rise again. Those who have done good will rise to eternal life, and those who have continued in evil will rise to judgement. ³⁰ But I do nothing without consulting the Father. I judge as I am told. And my judgement is absolutely just, because it is according to the will of God who sent me; it is not merely my own.

Witnesses to Jesus

[31] "If I were to testify on my own behalf, my testimony would not be valid. [32] But someone else is also testifying about me, and I can assure you that everything he says about me is true. [33] In fact, you sent messengers to listen to John the Baptist, and he preached the truth. [34] But the best testimony about me is not from a man, though I have reminded you about John's testimony so you might be saved. [35] John shone brightly for a while, and you benefited and rejoiced. [36] But I have a greater witness than John—my teachings and my miracles. They have been assigned to me by the Father, and they testify that the Father has sent me. [37] And the Father himself has also testified about me. You have never heard his voice or seen him face to face, [38] and you do not have his message in your hearts, because you do not believe me—the one he sent to you.

[39] "You search the Scriptures because you believe they give you eternal life. But the Scriptures point to me! [40] Yet you refuse to come to me so that I can give you this eternal life.

[41] "Your approval or disapproval means nothing to me, [42] because I know you don't have God's love within you. [43] For I have come to you representing my Father, and you refuse to welcome me, even though you readily accept others who represent only themselves. [44] No wonder you can't believe! For you gladly honour each other, but you don't care about the honour that comes from God alone.

[45] "Yet it is not I who will accuse you of this before the Father. Moses will accuse you! Yes, Moses, on whom you set your hopes. [46] But if you had believed Moses, you

would have believed me because he wrote about me. [47] And since you don't believe what he wrote, how will you believe what I say?"

CHAPTER 6

Jesus Feeds Five Thousand

After this, Jesus crossed over the Sea of Galilee, also known as the Sea of Tiberias. [2] And a huge crowd kept following him wherever he went, because they saw his miracles as he healed the sick. [3] Then Jesus went up into the hills and sat down with his disciples around him. [4] (It was nearly time for the annual Passover celebration.) [5] Jesus soon saw a great crowd of people climbing the hill, looking for him. Turning to Philip, he asked, "Philip, where can we buy bread to feed all these people?" [6] He was testing Philip, for he already knew what he was going to do.

[7] Philip replied, "It would take a small fortune* to feed them!"

[8] Then Andrew, Simon Peter's brother, spoke up. [9] "There's a young boy here with five barley loaves and two fish. But what good is that with this huge crowd?"

[10] "Tell everyone to sit down," Jesus ordered. So all of them—the men alone numbered five thousand—sat down on the grassy slopes. [11] Then Jesus took the loaves, gave thanks to God, and passed them out to the people. Afterwards he did the same with the fish. And they all ate until they were full. [12] "Now gather the leftovers," Jesus told his disciples, "so that nothing is wasted." [13] There were only five barley loaves to start with, but twelve

baskets were filled with the pieces of bread the people did not eat!

¹⁴ When the people saw this miraculous sign, they exclaimed, "Surely, he is the Prophet* we have been expecting!" ¹⁵ Jesus saw that they were ready to take him by force and make him king, so he went higher into the hills alone.

Jesus Walks on Water

¹⁶ That evening his disciples went down to the shore to wait for him. ¹⁷ But as darkness fell and Jesus still hadn't come back, they got into the boat and headed out across the lake towards Capernaum. ¹⁸ Soon a gale swept down upon them as they rowed, and the sea grew very rough. ¹⁹ They were five or six kilometres* out when suddenly they saw Jesus walking on the water towards the boat. They were terrified, ²⁰ but he called out to them, "I am here! Don't be afraid." ²¹ Then they were eager to let him in, and immediately the boat arrived at their destination!

Jesus, the Bread of Life

²² The next morning, back across the lake, crowds began gathering on the shore, waiting to see Jesus. For they knew that he and his disciples had come over together and that the disciples had gone off in their boat, leaving him behind. ²³ Several boats from Tiberias landed near the place where the Lord had blessed the bread and the people had eaten. ²⁴ When the crowd saw that Jesus wasn't there, nor his disciples, they got into the boats and went across to Capernaum to look for him. ²⁵ When they

arrived and found him, they asked, "Teacher, how did you get here?"

²⁶ Jesus replied, "The truth is, you want to be with me because I fed you, not because you saw the miraculous sign. ²⁷ But you shouldn't be so concerned about perishable things like food. Spend your energy seeking the eternal life that I, the Son of Man, can give you. For God the Father has sent me for that very purpose."

²⁸ They replied, "What does God want us to do?"

²⁹ Jesus told them, "This is what God wants you to do: Believe in the one he has sent."

³⁰ They replied, "You must show us a miraculous sign if you want us to believe in you. What will you do for us? ³¹ After all, our ancestors ate manna while they journeyed through the wilderness! As the Scriptures say, 'Moses gave them bread from heaven to eat.'*"

³² Jesus said, "I assure you, Moses didn't give them bread from heaven. My Father did. And now he offers you the true bread from heaven. ³³ The true bread of God is the one who comes down from heaven and gives life to the world."

³⁴ "Sir," they said, "give us that bread every day of our lives."

³⁵ Jesus replied, "I am the bread of life. No one who comes to me will ever be hungry again. Those who believe in me will never thirst. ³⁶ But you haven't believed in me even though you have seen me. ³⁷ However, those the Father has given me will come to me, and I will never reject them. ³⁸ For I have come down from heaven to do the will of God who sent me, not to do what I want. ³⁹ And this is the will of God, that I should not lose even one of all those he has given me, but that I should raise

them to eternal life at the last day. ⁴⁰For it is my Father's will that all who see his Son and believe in him should have eternal life—that I should raise them at the last day."

⁴¹Then the people* began to murmur in disagreement because he had said, "I am the bread from heaven." ⁴²They said, "This is Jesus, the son of Joseph. We know his father and mother. How can he say, 'I came down from heaven'?"

⁴³But Jesus replied, "Don't complain about what I said. ⁴⁴For people can't come to me unless the Father who sent me draws them to me, and at the last day I will raise them from the dead. ⁴⁵As it is written in the Scriptures, 'They will all be taught by God.'* Everyone who hears and learns from the Father comes to me. ⁴⁶(Not that anyone has ever seen the Father; only I, who was sent from God, have seen him.)

⁴⁷"I assure you, anyone who believes in me already has eternal life. ⁴⁸Yes, I am the bread of life! ⁴⁹Your ancestors ate manna in the wilderness, but they all died. ⁵⁰However, the bread from heaven gives eternal life to everyone who eats it. ⁵¹I am the living bread that came down out of heaven. Anyone who eats this bread will live for ever; this bread is my flesh, offered so the world may live."

⁵²Then the people began arguing with each other about what he meant. "How can this man give us his flesh to eat?" they asked.

⁵³So Jesus said again, "I assure you, unless you eat the flesh of the Son of Man and drink his blood, you cannot have eternal life within you. ⁵⁴But those who eat my flesh and drink my blood have eternal life, and I will raise them at the last day. ⁵⁵For my flesh is the true food, and my blood is the true drink. ⁵⁶All who eat my flesh and

drink my blood remain in me, and I in them. ⁵⁷I live by the power of the living Father who sent me; in the same way, those who partake of me will live because of me. ⁵⁸I am the true bread from heaven. Anyone who eats this bread will live for ever and not die as your ancestors did, even though they ate the manna."

⁵⁹He said these things while he was teaching in the synagogue in Capernaum.

Many Disciples Desert Jesus

⁶⁰Even his disciples said, "This is very hard to understand. How can anyone accept it?"

⁶¹Jesus knew within himself that his disciples were complaining, so he said to them, "Does this offend you? ⁶²Then what will you think if you see me, the Son of Man, return to heaven again? ⁶³It is the Spirit who gives eternal life. Human effort accomplishes nothing. And the very words I have spoken to you are spirit and life. ⁶⁴But some of you don't believe me." (For Jesus knew from the beginning who didn't believe, and he knew who would betray him.) ⁶⁵Then he said, "That is what I meant when I said that people can't come to me unless the Father brings them to me."

⁶⁶At this point many of his disciples turned away and deserted him. ⁶⁷Then Jesus turned to the Twelve and asked, "Are you going to leave, too?"

⁶⁸Simon Peter replied, "Lord, to whom would we go? You alone have the words that give eternal life. ⁶⁹We believe them, and we know you are the Holy One of God."

21

⁷⁰ Then Jesus said, "I chose the twelve of you, but one is a devil." ⁷¹ He was speaking of Judas, son of Simon Iscariot, one of the Twelve, who would betray him.

CHAPTER 7

Jesus and His Brothers

After this, Jesus stayed in Galilee, going from village to village. He wanted to stay out of Judea where the Jewish leaders were plotting his death. ² But soon it was time for the Festival of Shelters, ³ and Jesus' brothers urged him to go to Judea for the celebration. "Go where your followers can see your miracles!" they scoffed. ⁴ "You can't become a public figure if you hide like this! If you can do such wonderful things, prove it to the world!" ⁵ For even his brothers didn't believe in him.

⁶ Jesus replied, "Now is not the right time for me to go. But you can go any time, and it will make no difference. ⁷ The world can't hate you, but it does hate me because I accuse it of sin and evil. ⁸ You go on. I am not yet* ready to go to this festival, because my time has not yet come." ⁹ So Jesus remained in Galilee.

Jesus Teaches Openly at the Temple

¹⁰ But after his brothers had left for the festival, Jesus also went, though secretly, staying out of public view. ¹¹ The Jewish leaders tried to find him at the festival and kept asking if anyone had seen him. ¹² There was a lot of discussion about him among the crowds. Some said, "He's a wonderful man," while others said, "He's nothing but a

fraud, deceiving the people." [13]But no one had the courage to speak favourably about him in public, for they were afraid of getting into trouble with the Jewish leaders.

[14]Then, midway through the festival, Jesus went up to the Temple and began to teach. [15]The Jewish leaders were surprised when they heard him. "How does he know so much when he hasn't studied everything we've studied?" they asked.

[16]So Jesus told them, "I'm not teaching my own ideas, but those of God who sent me. [17]Anyone who wants to do the will of God will know whether my teaching is from God or is merely my own. [18]Those who present their own ideas are looking for praise for themselves, but those who seek to honour the one who sent them are good and genuine. [19]None of you obeys the law of Moses! In fact, you are trying to kill me."

[20]The crowd replied, "You're demon-possessed! Who's trying to kill you?"

[21]Jesus replied, "I worked on the Sabbath by healing a man, and you were offended. [22]But you work on the Sabbath, too, when you obey Moses' law of circumcision. (Actually, this tradition of circumcision is older than the law of Moses; it goes back to Abraham.) [23]For if the correct time for circumcising your son falls on the Sabbath, you go ahead and do it, so as not to break the law of Moses. So why should I be condemned for making a man completely well on the Sabbath? [24]Think this through and you will see that I am right."

Is Jesus the Messiah?

[25]Some of the people who lived there in Jerusalem said among themselves, "Isn't this the man they are trying to

kill? ²⁶But here he is, speaking in public, and they say nothing to him. Can it be that our leaders know that he really is the Messiah? ²⁷But how could he be? For we know where this man comes from. When the Messiah comes, he will simply appear; no one will know where he comes from."

²⁸While Jesus was teaching in the Temple, he called out, "Yes, you know me, and you know where I come from. But I represent one you don't know, and he is true. ²⁹I know him because I have come from him, and he sent me to you." ³⁰Then the leaders tried to arrest him; but no one laid a hand on him, because his time had not yet come.

³¹Many among the crowds at the Temple believed in him. "After all," they said, "would you expect the Messiah to do more miraculous signs than this man has done?"

³²When the Pharisees heard that the crowds were murmuring such things, they and the leading priests sent Temple guards to arrest Jesus. ³³But Jesus told them, "I will be here a little longer. Then I will return to the one who sent me. ³⁴You will search for me but not find me. And you won't be able to come where I am."

³⁵The Jewish leaders were puzzled by this statement. "Where is he planning to go?" they asked. "Maybe he is thinking of leaving the country and going to the Jews in other lands, or maybe even to the Gentiles! ³⁶What does he mean when he says, 'You will search for me but not find me,' and 'You won't be able to come where I am'?"

Jesus Promises Living Water

³⁷On the last day, the climax of the festival, Jesus stood and shouted to the crowds, "If you are thirsty, come to

me! [38] If you believe in me, come and drink! For the Scriptures declare that rivers of living water will flow out from within."* [39] (When he said "living water," he was speaking of the Spirit, who would be given to everyone believing in him. But the Spirit had not yet been given, because Jesus had not yet entered into his glory.)

Division and Unbelief

[40] When the crowds heard him say this, some of them declared, "This man surely is the Prophet."* [41] Others said, "He is the Messiah." Still others said, "But he can't be! Will the Messiah come from Galilee? [42] For the Scriptures clearly state that the Messiah will be born of the royal line of David, in Bethlehem, the village where King David was born."* [43] So the crowd was divided in their opinion about him. [44] And some wanted him arrested, but no one touched him.

[45] The Temple guards who had been sent to arrest him returned to the leading priests and Pharisees. "Why didn't you bring him in?" they demanded.

[46] "We have never heard anyone talk like this!" the guards responded.

[47] "Have you been led astray, too?" the Pharisees mocked. [48] "Is there a single one of us rulers or Pharisees who believes in him? [49] These ignorant crowds do, but what do they know about it? A curse on them anyway!"

[50] Nicodemus, the leader who had met with Jesus earlier, then spoke up. [51] "Is it legal to convict a man before he is given a hearing?" he asked.

[52] They replied, "Are you from Galilee, too? Search the Scriptures and see for yourself—no prophet ever comes from Galilee!"

[*The most ancient Greek manuscripts do not include John 7:53–8:11.*]

⁵³ Then the meeting broke up and everybody went home.

CHAPTER 8

A Woman Caught in Adultery

Jesus returned to the Mount of Olives, ²but early the next morning he was back again at the Temple. A crowd soon gathered, and he sat down and taught them. ³As he was speaking, the teachers of religious law and Pharisees brought a woman they had caught in the act of adultery. They put her in front of the crowd.

⁴"Teacher," they said to Jesus, "this woman was caught in the very act of adultery. ⁵The law of Moses says to stone her. What do you say?"

⁶They were trying to trap him into saying something they could use against him, but Jesus stooped down and wrote in the dust with his finger. ⁷They kept demanding an answer, so he stood up again and said, "All right, stone her. But let those who have never sinned throw the first stones!" ⁸Then he stooped down again and wrote in the dust.

⁹When the accusers heard this, they slipped away one by one, beginning with the oldest, until only Jesus was left in the middle of the crowd with the woman. ¹⁰Then Jesus stood up again and said to her, "Where are your accusers? Didn't even one of them condemn you?"

¹¹"No, Lord," she said.

And Jesus said, "Neither do I. Go and sin no more."

Jesus, the Light of the World

¹² Jesus said to the people, "I am the light of the world. If you follow me, you won't be stumbling through the darkness, because you will have the light that leads to life."

¹³ The Pharisees replied, "You are making false claims about yourself!"

¹⁴ Jesus told them, "These claims are valid even though I make them about myself. For I know where I came from and where I am going, but you don't know this about me. ¹⁵ You judge me with all your human limitations,* but I am not judging anyone. ¹⁶ And if I did, my judgement would be correct in every respect because I am not alone—I have with me the Father who sent me. ¹⁷ Your own law says that if two people agree about something, their witness is accepted as fact.* ¹⁸ I am one witness, and my Father who sent me is the other."

¹⁹ "Where is your father?" they asked.

Jesus answered, "Since you don't know who I am, you don't know who my Father is. If you knew me, then you would know my Father, too." ²⁰ Jesus made these statements while he was teaching in the section of the Temple known as the Treasury. But he was not arrested, because his time had not yet come.

The Unbelieving People Warned

²¹ Later Jesus said to them again, "I am going away. You will search for me and die in your sin. You cannot come where I am going."

²² The Jewish leaders asked, "Is he planning to commit suicide? What does he mean, 'You cannot come where I am going'?"

27

²³ Then he said to them, "You are from below; I am from above. You are of this world; I am not. ²⁴ That is why I said that you will die in your sins; for unless you believe that I am who I say I am, you will die in your sins."

²⁵ "Tell us who you are," they demanded.

Jesus replied, "I am the one I have always claimed to be.* ²⁶ I have much to say about you and much to condemn, but I won't. For I say only what I have heard from the one who sent me, and he is true." ²⁷ But they still didn't understand that he was talking to them about his Father.

²⁸ So Jesus said, "When you have lifted up the Son of Man on the cross, then you will realize that I am he and that I do nothing on my own, but I speak what the Father taught me. ²⁹ And the one who sent me is with me—he has not deserted me. For I always do those things that are pleasing to him." ³⁰ Then many who heard him say these things believed in him.

Jesus and Abraham

³¹ Jesus said to the people* who believed in him, "You are truly my disciples if you keep obeying my teachings. ³² And you will know the truth, and the truth will set you free."

³³ "But we are descendants of Abraham," they said. "We have never been slaves to anyone on earth. What do you mean, 'set free'?"

³⁴ Jesus replied, "I assure you that everyone who sins is a slave of sin. ³⁵ A slave is not a permanent member of the family, but a son is part of the family for ever. ³⁶ So if the Son sets you free, you will indeed be free. ³⁷ Yes, I realize that you are descendants of Abraham. And yet some of

you are trying to kill me because my message does not find a place in your hearts. [38] I am telling you what I saw when I was with my Father. But you are following the advice of your father."

[39] "Our father is Abraham," they declared.

"No," Jesus replied, "for if you were children of Abraham, you would follow his good example.* [40] I told you the truth I heard from God, but you are trying to kill me. Abraham wouldn't do a thing like that. [41] No, you are obeying your real father when you act that way."

They replied, "We were not born out of wedlock! Our true Father is God himself."

[42] Jesus told them, "If God were your Father, you would love me, because I have come to you from God. I am not here on my own, but he sent me. [43] Why can't you understand what I am saying? It is because you are unable to do so! [44] For you are the children of your father the Devil, and you love to do the evil things he does. He was a murderer from the beginning and has always hated the truth. There is no truth in him. When he lies, it is consistent with his character; for he is a liar and the father of lies. [45] So when I tell the truth, you just naturally don't believe me! [46] Which of you can truthfully accuse me of sin? And since I am telling you the truth, why don't you believe me? [47] Anyone whose Father is God listens gladly to the words of God. Since you don't, it proves you aren't God's children."

[48] The people retorted, "You Samaritan devil! Didn't we say all along that you were possessed by a demon?"

[49] "No," Jesus said, "I have no demon in me. For I honour my Father—and you dishonour me. [50] And though I have no wish to glorify myself, God wants to glorify me.

Let him be the judge. ⁵¹ I assure you, anyone who obeys my teaching will never die!"

⁵² The people said, "Now we know you are possessed by a demon. Even Abraham and the prophets died, but you say that those who obey your teaching will never die! ⁵³ Are you greater than our father Abraham, who died? Are you greater than the prophets, who died? Who do you think you are?"

⁵⁴ Jesus answered, "If I am merely boasting about myself, it doesn't count. But it is my Father who says these glorious things about me. You say, 'He is our God,' ⁵⁵ but you do not even know him. I know him. If I said otherwise, I would be as great a liar as you! But it is true—I know him and obey him. ⁵⁶ Your ancestor Abraham rejoiced as he looked forward to my coming. He saw it and was glad."

⁵⁷ The people said, "You aren't even fifty years old. How can you say you have seen Abraham?*"

⁵⁸ Jesus answered, "The truth is, I existed before Abraham was even born!"* ⁵⁹ At that point they picked up stones to kill him. But Jesus hid himself from them and left the Temple.

CHAPTER 9

Jesus Heals a Man Born Blind

As Jesus was walking along, he saw a man who had been blind from birth. ² "Teacher," his disciples asked him, "why was this man born blind? Was it a result of his own sins or those of his parents?"

³ "It was not because of his sins or his parents' sins," Jesus answered. "He was born blind so the power of God could be seen in him. ⁴ All of us must quickly carry out the tasks assigned us by the one who sent me, because there is little time left before the night falls and all work comes to an end. ⁵ But while I am still here in the world, I am the light of the world."

⁶ Then he spat on the ground, made mud with the saliva, and smoothed the mud over the blind man's eyes. ⁷ He told him, "Go and wash in the pool of Siloam" (Siloam means Sent). So the man went and washed, and came back seeing!

⁸ His neighbours and others who knew him as a blind beggar asked each other, "Is this the same man—that beggar?" ⁹ Some said he was, and others said, "No, but he surely looks like him!"

And the beggar kept saying, "I am the same man!"

¹⁰ They asked, "Who healed you? What happened?"

¹¹ He told them, "The man they call Jesus made mud and smoothed it over my eyes and told me, 'Go to the pool of Siloam and wash off the mud.' I went and washed, and now I can see!"

¹² "Where is he now?" they asked.

"I don't know," he replied.

¹³ Then they took the man to the Pharisees. ¹⁴ Now as it happened, Jesus had healed the man on a Sabbath. ¹⁵ The Pharisees asked the man all about it. So he told them, "He smoothed the mud over my eyes, and when it was washed away, I could see!"

¹⁶ Some of the Pharisees said, "This man Jesus is not from God, for he is working on the Sabbath." Others said, "But how could an ordinary sinner do such

miraculous signs?" So there was a deep division of opinion among them.

¹⁷ Then the Pharisees once again questioned the man who had been blind and demanded, "This man who opened your eyes—who do you say he is?"

The man replied, "I think he must be a prophet."

¹⁸ The Jewish leaders wouldn't believe he had been blind, so they called in his parents. ¹⁹ They asked them, "Is this your son? Was he born blind? If so, how can he see?"

²⁰ His parents replied, "We know this is our son and that he was born blind, ²¹ but we don't know how he can see or who healed him. He is old enough to speak for himself. Ask him." ²² They said this because they were afraid of the Jewish leaders, who had announced that anyone saying Jesus was the Messiah would be expelled from the synagogue. ²³ That's why they said, "He is old enough to speak for himself. Ask him."

²⁴ So for the second time they called in the man who had been blind and told him, "Give glory to God by telling the truth,* because we know Jesus is a sinner."

²⁵ "I don't know whether he is a sinner," the man replied. "But I know this: I was blind, and now I can see!"

²⁶ "But what did he do?" they asked. "How did he heal you?"

²⁷ "Look!" the man exclaimed. "I told you once. Didn't you listen? Why do you want to hear it again? Do you want to become his disciples, too?"

²⁸ Then they cursed him and said, "You are his disciple, but we are disciples of Moses. ²⁹ We know God spoke to Moses, but as for this man, we don't know anything about him."

³⁰ "Why, that's very strange!" the man replied. "He healed my eyes, and yet you don't know anything about him! ³¹ Well, God doesn't listen to sinners, but he is ready to hear those who worship him and do his will. ³² Never since the world began has anyone been able to open the eyes of someone born blind. ³³ If this man were not from God, he couldn't do it."

³⁴ "You were born in sin!" they answered. "Are you trying to teach us?" And they threw him out of the synagogue.

Spiritual Blindness

³⁵ When Jesus heard what had happened, he found the man and said, "Do you believe in the Son of Man*?"

³⁶ The man answered, "Who is he, sir? I want to believe in him."

³⁷ "You have seen him," Jesus said, "and he is speaking to you!"

³⁸ "Yes, Lord," the man said, "I believe!" And he worshipped Jesus.

³⁹ Then Jesus told him, "I have come to judge the world. I have come to give sight to the blind and to show those who think they see that they are blind."

⁴⁰ The Pharisees who were standing there heard him and asked, "Are you saying we are blind?"

⁴¹ "If you were blind, you wouldn't be guilty," Jesus replied. "But you remain guilty because you claim you can see.

CHAPTER 10

The Good Shepherd and His Sheep

"I assure you, anyone who sneaks over the wall of a sheepfold, rather than going through the gate, must surely be a thief and a robber! [2] For a shepherd enters through the gate. [3] The gatekeeper opens the gate for him, and the sheep hear his voice and come to him. He calls his own sheep by name and leads them out. [4] After he has gathered his own flock, he walks ahead of them, and they follow him because they recognize his voice. [5] They won't follow a stranger; they will run from him because they don't recognize his voice."

[6] Those who heard Jesus use this illustration didn't understand what he meant, [7] so he explained it to them. "I assure you, I am the gate for the sheep," he said. [8] "All others who came before me were thieves and robbers. But the true sheep did not listen to them. [9] Yes, I am the gate. Those who come in through me will be saved. Wherever they go, they will find green pastures. [10] The thief's purpose is to steal and kill and destroy. My purpose is to give life in all its fullness.

[11] "I am the good shepherd. The good shepherd lays down his life for the sheep. [12] A hired hand will run when he sees a wolf coming. He will leave the sheep because they aren't his and he isn't their shepherd. And so the wolf attacks them and scatters the flock. [13] The hired hand runs away because he is merely hired and has no real concern for the sheep.

[14] "I am the good shepherd; I know my own sheep, and they know me, [15] just as my Father knows me and I know

the Father. And I lay down my life for the sheep. [16] I have other sheep, too, that are not in this sheepfold. I must bring them also, and they will listen to my voice; and there will be one flock with one shepherd.

[17] "The Father loves me because I lay down my life that I may have it back again. [18] No one can take my life from me. I lay down my life voluntarily. For I have the right to lay it down when I want to and also the power to take it again. For my Father has given me this command."

[19] When he said these things, the people* were again divided in their opinions about him. [20] Some of them said, "He has a demon, or he's crazy. Why listen to a man like that?" [21] Others said, "This doesn't sound like a man possessed by a demon! Can a demon open the eyes of the blind?"

Jesus Claims to Be the Son of God

[22] It was now winter, and Jesus was in Jerusalem at the time of Hanukkah.* [23] He was at the Temple, walking through the section known as Solomon's Colonnade. [24] The Jewish leaders surrounded him and asked, "How long are you going to keep us in suspense? If you are the Messiah, tell us plainly."

[25] Jesus replied, "I have already told you, and you don't believe me. The proof is what I do in the name of my Father. [26] But you don't believe me because you are not part of my flock. [27] My sheep recognize my voice; I know them, and they follow me. [28] I give them eternal life, and they will never perish. No one will snatch them away from me, [29] for my Father has given them to me, and he is more powerful than anyone else. So no one can take them from me. [30] The Father and I are one."

[31] Once again the Jewish leaders picked up stones to kill him. [32] Jesus said, "At my Father's direction I have done many things to help the people. For which one of these good deeds are you killing me?"

[33] They replied, "Not for any good work, but for blasphemy, because you, a mere man, have made yourself God."

[34] Jesus replied, "It is written in your own law that God said to certain leaders of the people, 'I say, you are gods!'* [35] And you know that the Scriptures cannot be altered. So if those people, who received God's message, were called 'gods,' [36] why do you call it blasphemy when the Holy One who was sent into the world by the Father says, 'I am the Son of God'? [37] Don't believe me unless I carry out my Father's work. [38] But if I do his work, believe in what I have done, even if you don't believe me. Then you will realize that the Father is in me, and I am in the Father."

[39] Once again they tried to arrest him, but he got away and left them. [40] He went beyond the River Jordan to stay near the place where John was first baptizing. [41] And many followed him. "John didn't do miracles," they remarked to one another, "but all his predictions about this man have come true." [42] And many believed in him there.

CHAPTER 11

The Death of Lazarus

A man named Lazarus was sick. He lived in Bethany with his sisters, Mary and Martha. [2] This is the Mary who poured the expensive perfume on the Lord's feet and wiped them with her hair.* Her brother, Lazarus, was sick. ³ So the two sisters sent a message to Jesus telling him, "Lord, the one you love is very sick."

⁴ But when Jesus heard about it he said, "Lazarus's sickness will not end in death. No, it is for the glory of God. I, the Son of God, will receive glory from this." ⁵ Although Jesus loved Martha, Mary, and Lazarus, ⁶ he stayed where he was for the next two days and did not go to them. ⁷ Finally after two days, he said to his disciples, "Let's go to Judea again."

⁸ But his disciples objected. "Teacher," they said, "only a few days ago the Jewish leaders in Judea were trying to kill you. Are you going there again?"

⁹ Jesus replied, "There are twelve hours of daylight every day. As long as it is light, people can walk safely. They can see because they have the light of this world. ¹⁰ Only at night is there danger of stumbling because there is no light." ¹¹ Then he said, "Our friend Lazarus has fallen asleep, but now I will go and wake him up."

¹² The disciples said, "Lord, if he is sleeping, that means he is getting better!" ¹³ They thought Jesus meant Lazarus was having a good night's rest, but Jesus meant Lazarus had died.

¹⁴ Then he told them plainly, "Lazarus is dead. ¹⁵ And for your sake, I am glad I wasn't there, because this will give you another opportunity to believe in me. Come, let's go and see him."

¹⁶ Thomas, nicknamed the Twin,* said to his fellow disciples, "Let's go, too—and die with Jesus."

¹⁷ When Jesus arrived at Bethany, he was told that Lazarus had already been in his grave for four days. ¹⁸ Bethany was only about three kilometres* down the road from Jerusalem, ¹⁹ and many of the people* had

come to pay their respects and console Martha and Mary on their loss. ²⁰ When Martha got word that Jesus was coming, she went to meet him. But Mary stayed at home. ²¹ Martha said to Jesus, "Lord, if you had been here, my brother would not have died. ²² But even now I know that God will give you whatever you ask."

²³ Jesus told her, "Your brother will rise again."

²⁴ "Yes," Martha said, "when everyone else rises, on resurrection day."

²⁵ Jesus told her, "I am the resurrection and the life.* Those who believe in me, even though they die like everyone else, will live again. ²⁶ They are given eternal life for believing in me and will never perish. Do you believe this, Martha?"

²⁷ "Yes, Lord," she told him. "I have always believed you are the Messiah, the Son of God, the one who has come into the world from God." ²⁸ Then she left him and returned to Mary. She called Mary aside from the mourners and told her, "The Teacher is here and wants to see you." ²⁹ So Mary immediately went to him.

³⁰ Now Jesus had stayed outside the village, at the place where Martha met him. ³¹ When the people who were at the house trying to console Mary saw her leave so hastily, they assumed she was going to Lazarus's grave to weep. So they followed her there. ³² When Mary arrived and saw Jesus, she fell down at his feet and said, "Lord, if you had been here, my brother would not have died."

³³ When Jesus saw her weeping and saw the other people wailing with her, he was moved with indignation and was deeply troubled. ³⁴ "Where have you put him?" he asked them.

They told him, "Lord, come and see." [35] Then Jesus wept. [36] The people who were standing nearby said, "See how much he loved him." [37] But some said, "This man healed a blind man. Why couldn't he keep Lazarus from dying?"

Jesus Raises Lazarus from the Dead

[38] And again Jesus was deeply troubled. Then they came to the grave. It was a cave with a stone rolled across its entrance. [39] "Roll the stone aside," Jesus told them.

But Martha, the dead man's sister, said, "Lord, by now the smell will be terrible because he has been dead for four days."

[40] Jesus responded, "Didn't I tell you that you will see God's glory if you believe?" [41] So they rolled the stone aside. Then Jesus looked up to heaven and said, "Father, thank you for hearing me. [42] You always hear me, but I said it out loud for the sake of all these people standing here, so they will believe you sent me." [43] Then Jesus shouted, "Lazarus, come out!" [44] And Lazarus came out, bound in graveclothes, his face wrapped in a headcloth. Jesus told them, "Unwrap him and let him go!"

The Plot to Kill Jesus

[45] Many of the people who were with Mary believed in Jesus when they saw this happen. [46] But some went to the Pharisees and told them what Jesus had done. [47] Then the leading priests and Pharisees called the high council* together to discuss the situation. "What are we going to do?" they asked each other. "This man certainly performs many miraculous signs. [48] If we leave him alone,

the whole nation will follow him, and then the Roman army will come and destroy both our Temple and our nation."

⁴⁹ And one of them, Caiaphas, who was high priest that year, said, "How can you be so stupid? ⁵⁰ Why should the whole nation be destroyed? Let this one man die for the people."

⁵¹ This prophecy that Jesus should die for the entire nation came from Caiaphas in his position as high priest. He didn't think of it himself; he was inspired to say it. ⁵² It was a prediction that Jesus' death would be not for Israel only, but for the gathering together of all the children of God scattered around the world.

⁵³ So from that time on the Jewish leaders began to plot Jesus' death. ⁵⁴ As a result, Jesus stopped his public ministry among the people and left Jerusalem. He went to a place near the wilderness, to the village of Ephraim, and stayed there with his disciples.

⁵⁵ It was now almost time for the celebration of Passover, and many people from the country arrived in Jerusalem several days early so they could go through the cleansing ceremony before the Passover began. ⁵⁶ They wanted to see Jesus, and as they talked in the Temple, they asked each other, "What do you think? Will he come for the Passover?" ⁵⁷ Meanwhile, the leading priests and Pharisees had publicly announced that anyone seeing Jesus must report him immediately so they could arrest him.

CHAPTER 12

Jesus Anointed at Bethany

Six days before the Passover ceremonies began, Jesus arrived in Bethany, the home of Lazarus—the man he had raised from the dead. ²A dinner was prepared in Jesus' honour. Martha served, and Lazarus sat at the table with him. ³Then Mary took more than three hundred grams* of expensive perfume made from essence of nard, and she anointed Jesus' feet with it and wiped his feet with her hair. And the house was filled with fragrance.

⁴But Judas Iscariot, one of his disciples—the one who would betray him—said, ⁵"That perfume was worth a small fortune.* It should have been sold and the money given to the poor." ⁶Not that he cared for the poor—he was a thief who was in charge of the disciples' funds, and he often took some for his own use.

⁷Jesus replied, "Leave her alone. She did it in preparation for my burial. ⁸You will always have the poor among you, but I will not be here with you much longer."

⁹When all the people* heard of Jesus' arrival, they flocked to see him and also to see Lazarus, the man Jesus had raised from the dead. ¹⁰Then the leading priests decided to kill Lazarus, too, ¹¹for it was because of him that many of the people had deserted them and believed in Jesus.

The Triumphal Entry

¹²The next day, the news that Jesus was on the way to Jerusalem swept through the city. A huge crowd of

Passover visitors [13] took palm branches and went down the road to meet him. They shouted,

"Praise God!*ª

Bless the one who comes in the name of the Lord!

Hail to the King of Israel!"*ᵇ

[14] Jesus found a young donkey and sat on it, fulfilling the prophecy that said:

[15] "Don't be afraid, people of Israel.*ª

Look, your King is coming,

sitting on a donkey's colt."*ᵇ

[16] His disciples didn't realize at the time that this was a fulfilment of prophecy. But after Jesus entered into his glory, they remembered that these Scriptures had come true before their eyes.

[17] Those in the crowd who had seen Jesus call Lazarus back to life were telling others all about it. [18] That was the main reason so many went out to meet him—because they had heard about this mighty miracle. [19] Then the Pharisees said to each other, "We've lost. Look, the whole world has gone after him!"

Jesus Predicts His Death

[20] Some Greeks who had come to Jerusalem to attend the Passover [21] paid a visit to Philip, who was from Bethsaida in Galilee. They said, "Sir, we want to meet Jesus." [22] Philip told Andrew about it, and they went together to ask Jesus.

[23] Jesus replied, "The time has come for the Son of Man to enter into his glory. [24] The truth is, a kernel of wheat must be planted in the soil. Unless it dies it will be alone—a single seed. But its death will produce many new kernels—a plentiful harvest of new lives. [25] Those

who love their life in this world will lose it. Those who despise their life in this world will keep it for eternal life. [26] All those who want to be my disciples must come and follow me, because my servants must be where I am. And if they follow me, the Father will honour them. [27] Now my soul is deeply troubled. Should I pray, 'Father, save me from what lies ahead'? But that is the very reason why I came! [28] Father, bring glory to your name."

Then a voice spoke from heaven, saying, "I have already brought it glory, and I will do it again." [29] When the crowd heard the voice, some thought it was thunder, while others declared an angel had spoken to him. [30] Then Jesus told them, "The voice was for your benefit, not mine. [31] The time of judgement for the world has come, when the prince of this world* will be cast out. [32] And when I am lifted up on the cross,* I will draw everyone to myself." [33] He said this to indicate how he was going to die.

[34] "Die?" asked the crowd. "We understood from Scripture that the Messiah would live for ever. Why are you saying the Son of Man will die? Who is this Son of Man you are talking about?"

[35] Jesus replied, "My light will shine out for you just a little while longer. Walk in it while you can, so you will not stumble when the darkness falls. If you walk in the darkness, you cannot see where you are going. [36] Believe in the light while there is still time; then you will become children of the light." After saying these things, Jesus went away and was hidden from them.

The Unbelief of the People

[37] But despite all the miraculous signs he had done, most of the people did not believe in him. [38] This is exactly what Isaiah the prophet had predicted:

"Lord, who has believed our message?
　　To whom will the Lord reveal his saving power?"*
[39] But the people couldn't believe, for as Isaiah also said,
[40] "The Lord has blinded their eyes
　　and hardened their hearts—
so their eyes cannot see,
　　and their hearts cannot understand,
and they cannot turn to me
　　and let me heal them."*

[41] Isaiah was referring to Jesus when he made this prediction, because he was given a vision of the Messiah's glory. [42] Many people, including some of the Jewish leaders, believed in him. But they wouldn't admit it to anyone because of their fear that the Pharisees would expel them from the synagogue. [43] For they loved human praise more than the praise of God.

[44] Jesus shouted to the crowds, "If you trust me, you are really trusting God who sent me. [45] For when you see me, you are seeing the one who sent me. [46] I have come as a light to shine in this dark world, so that all who put their trust in me will no longer remain in the darkness. [47] If anyone hears me and doesn't obey me, I am not his judge—for I have come to save the world and not to judge it. [48] But all who reject me and my message will be judged at the day of judgement by the truth I have spoken. [49] I don't speak on my own authority. The Father who sent me gave me his own instructions as to what I

should say. ⁵⁰ And I know his instructions lead to eternal life; so I say whatever the Father tells me to say!"

CHAPTER 13

Jesus Washes His Disciples' Feet

Before the Passover celebration, Jesus knew that his hour had come to leave this world and return to his Father. He now showed the disciples the full extent of his love.* ² It was time for supper, and the Devil had already enticed Judas, son of Simon Iscariot, to carry out his plan to betray Jesus. ³ Jesus knew that the Father had given him authority over everything and that he had come from God and would return to God. ⁴ So he got up from the table, took off his robe, wrapped a towel around his waist, ⁵ and poured water into a basin. Then he began to wash the disciples' feet and to wipe them with the towel he had around him.

⁶ When he came to Simon Peter, Peter said to him, "Lord, why are you going to wash my feet?"

⁷ Jesus replied, "You don't understand now why I am doing it; someday you will."

⁸ "No," Peter protested, "you will never wash my feet!"

Jesus replied, "But if I don't wash you, you won't belong to me."

⁹ Simon Peter exclaimed, "Then wash my hands and head as well, Lord, not just my feet!"

¹⁰ Jesus replied, "A person who has bathed all over does not need to wash, except for the feet,* to be entirely clean. And you are clean, but that isn't true of everyone

here." [11] For Jesus knew who would betray him. That is what he meant when he said, "Not all of you are clean."

[12] After washing their feet, he put on his robe again and sat down and asked, "Do you understand what I was doing? [13] You call me 'Teacher' and 'Lord,' and you are right, because it is true. [14] And since I, the Lord and Teacher, have washed your feet, you ought to wash each other's feet. [15] I have given you an example to follow. Do as I have done to you. [16] How true it is that a servant is not greater than the master. Nor are messengers more important than the one who sends them. [17] You know these things—now do them! That is the path of blessing.

Jesus Predicts His Betrayal

[18] "I am not saying these things to all of you; I know so well each one of you I chose. The Scriptures declare, 'The one who shares my food has turned against me,'* and this will soon come true. [19] I tell you this now, so that when it happens you will believe I am the Messiah. [20] Truly, anyone who welcomes my messenger is welcoming me, and anyone who welcomes me is welcoming the Father who sent me."

[21] Now Jesus was in great anguish of spirit, and he exclaimed, "The truth is, one of you will betray me!"

[22] The disciples looked at each other, wondering whom he could mean. [23] One of Jesus' disciples, the one Jesus loved, was sitting next to Jesus at the table.* [24] Simon Peter motioned to him to ask who would do this terrible thing. [25] Leaning towards Jesus, he asked, "Lord, who is it?"

[26] Jesus said, "It is the one to whom I give the bread dipped in the sauce." And when he had dipped it, he gave it to Judas, son of Simon Iscariot. [27] As soon as

Judas had eaten the bread, Satan entered into him. Then Jesus told him, "Hurry. Do it now." ²⁸ None of the others at the table knew what Jesus meant. ²⁹ Since Judas was their treasurer, some thought Jesus was telling him to go and pay for the food or to give some money to the poor. ³⁰ So Judas left at once, going out into the night.

Jesus Predicts Peter's Denial

³¹ As soon as Judas left the room, Jesus said, "The time has come for me, the Son of Man, to enter into my glory, and God will receive glory because of all that happens to me. ³² And God will bring* me into my glory very soon. ³³ Dear children, how brief are these moments before I must go away and leave you! Then, though you search for me, you cannot come to me—just as I told the Jewish leaders. ³⁴ So now I am giving you a new commandment: Love each other. Just as I have loved you, you should love each other. ³⁵ Your love for one another will prove to the world that you are my disciples."

³⁶ Simon Peter said, "Lord, where are you going?"

And Jesus replied, "You can't go with me now, but you will follow me later."

³⁷ "But why can't I come now, Lord?" he asked. "I am ready to die for you."

³⁸ Jesus answered, "Die for me? No, before the cock crows tomorrow morning, you will deny three times that you even know me.

47

CHAPTER 14

Jesus, the Way to the Father

"Don't be troubled. You trust God, now trust in me. ²There are many rooms in my Father's home, and I am going to prepare a place for you. If this were not so, I would tell you plainly. ³When everything is ready, I will come and get you, so that you will always be with me where I am. ⁴And you know where I am going and how to get there."

⁵"No, we don't know, Lord," Thomas said. "We haven't any idea where you are going, so how can we know the way?"

⁶Jesus told him, "I am the way, the truth, and the life. No one can come to the Father except through me. ⁷If you had known who I am, then you would have known who my Father is.* From now on you know him and have seen him!"

⁸Philip said, "Lord, show us the Father and we will be satisfied."

⁹Jesus replied, "Philip, don't you even yet know who I am, even after all the time I have been with you? Anyone who has seen me has seen the Father! So why are you asking to see him? ¹⁰Don't you believe that I am in the Father and the Father is in me? The words I say are not my own, but my Father who lives in me does his work through me. ¹¹Just believe that I am in the Father and the Father is in me. Or at least believe because of what you have seen me do.

¹²"The truth is, anyone who believes in me will do the same works I have done, and even greater works,

because I am going to be with the Father. ¹³ You can ask for anything in my name, and I will do it, because the work of the Son brings glory to the Father. ¹⁴ Yes, ask anything in my name, and I will do it!

Jesus Promises the Holy Spirit

¹⁵ "If you love me, obey my commandments. ¹⁶ And I will ask the Father, and he will give you another Counsellor,* who will never leave you. ¹⁷ He is the Holy Spirit, who leads into all truth. The world at large cannot receive him, because it isn't looking for him and doesn't recognize him. But you do, because he lives with you now and later will be in you. ¹⁸ No, I will not abandon you as orphans—I will come to you. ¹⁹ In just a little while the world will not see me again, but you will. For I will live again, and you will, too. ²⁰ When I am raised to life again, you will know that I am in my Father, and you are in me, and I am in you. ²¹ Those who obey my commandments are the ones who love me. And because they love me, my Father will love them, and I will love them. And I will reveal myself to each one of them."

²² Judas (not Judas Iscariot, but the other disciple with that name) said to him, "Lord, why are you going to reveal yourself only to us and not to the world at large?"

²³ Jesus replied, "All those who love me will do what I say. My Father will love them, and we will come to them and live with them. ²⁴ Anyone who doesn't love me will not do what I say. And remember, my words are not my own. This message is from the Father who sent me. ²⁵ I am telling you these things now while I am still with you. ²⁶ But when the Father sends the Counsellor as my representative—and by the Counsellor I mean the Holy

Spirit—he will teach you everything and will remind you of everything I myself have told you.

²⁷"I am leaving you with a gift—peace of mind and heart. And the peace I give isn't like the peace the world gives. So don't be troubled or afraid. ²⁸Remember what I told you: I am going away, but I will come back to you again. If you really love me, you will be very happy for me, because now I can go to the Father, who is greater than I am. ²⁹I have told you these things before they happen so that you will believe when they do happen.

³⁰"I don't have much more time to talk to you, because the prince of this world approaches. He has no power over me, ³¹but I will do what the Father requires of me, so that the world will know that I love the Father. Come, let's be going.

CHAPTER 15

Jesus, the True Vine

"I am the true vine, and my Father is the gardener. ²He cuts off every branch that doesn't produce fruit, and he prunes the branches that do bear fruit so they will produce even more. ³You have already been pruned for greater fruitfulness by the message I have given you. ⁴Remain in me, and I will remain in you. For a branch cannot produce fruit if it is severed from the vine, and you cannot be fruitful apart from me.

⁵"Yes, I am the vine; you are the branches. Those who remain in me, and I in them, will produce much fruit. For apart from me you can do nothing. ⁶Anyone who parts from me is thrown away like a useless branch and

withers. Such branches are gathered into a pile to be burned. [7] But if you stay joined to me and my words remain in you, you may ask any request you like, and it will be granted! [8] My true disciples produce much fruit. This brings great glory to my Father.

[9] "I have loved you even as the Father has loved me. Remain in my love. [10] When you obey me, you remain in my love, just as I obey my Father and remain in his love. [11] I have told you this so that you will be filled with my joy. Yes, your joy will overflow! [12] I command you to love each other in the same way that I love you. [13] And here is how to measure it—the greatest love is shown when people lay down their lives for their friends. [14] You are my friends if you obey me. [15] I no longer call you servants, because a master doesn't confide in his servants. Now you are my friends, since I have told you everything the Father told me. [16] You didn't choose me. I chose you. I appointed you to go and produce fruit that will last, so that the Father will give you whatever you ask for, using my name. [17] I command you to love each other.

The World's Hatred

[18] "When the world hates you, remember it hated me before it hated you. [19] The world would love you if you belonged to it, but you don't. I chose you to come out of the world, and so it hates you. [20] Do you remember what I told you? 'A servant is not greater than the master.' Since they persecuted me, naturally they will persecute you. And if they had listened to me, they would listen to you! [21] The people of the world will hate you because you belong to me, for they don't know God who sent me. [22] They would not be guilty if I had not come and spoken

to them. But now they have no excuse for their sin. [23] Anyone who hates me hates my Father, too. [24] If I hadn't done such miraculous signs among them that no one else could do, they would not be counted guilty. But as it is, they saw all that I did and yet hated both of us—me and my Father. [25] This has fulfilled what the Scriptures said: 'They hated me without cause.'*

[26] "But I will send you the Counsellor*—the Spirit of truth. He will come to you from the Father and will tell you all about me. [27] And you must also tell others about me because you have been with me from the beginning.

CHAPTER 16

"I have told you these things so that you won't fall away. [2] For you will be expelled from the synagogues, and the time is coming when those who kill you will think they are doing God a service. [3] This is because they have never known the Father or me. [4] Yes, I'm telling you these things now, so that when they happen, you will remember I warned you. I didn't tell you earlier because I was going to be with you for a while longer.

The Work of the Holy Spirit

[5] "But now I am going away to the one who sent me, and none of you has asked me where I am going. [6] Instead, you are very sad. [7] But it is actually best for you that I go away, because if I don't, the Counsellor* won't come. If I do go away, he will come because I will send him to you. [8] And when he comes, he will convince the world of its sin, and of God's righteousness, and of the coming judgement. [9] The

world's sin is unbelief in me. [10]Righteousness is available because I go to the Father, and you will see me no more. [11]Judgement will come because the prince of this world has already been judged.

[12]"Oh, there is so much more I want to tell you, but you can't bear it now. [13]When the Spirit of truth comes, he will guide you into all truth. He will not be presenting his own ideas; he will be telling you what he has heard. He will tell you about the future. [14]He will bring me glory by revealing to you whatever he receives from me. [15]All that the Father has is mine; this is what I mean when I say that the Spirit will reveal to you whatever he receives from me.

Sadness Will Be Turned to Joy

[16]"In just a little while I will be gone, and you won't see me any more. Then, just a little while after that, you will see me again."

[17]The disciples asked each other, "What does he mean when he says, 'You won't see me, and then you will see me'? And what does he mean when he says, 'I am going to the Father'? [18]And what does he mean by 'a little while'? We don't understand."

[19]Jesus realized they wanted to ask him, so he said, "Are you asking yourselves what I meant? I said in just a little while I will be gone, and you won't see me any more. Then, just a little while after that, you will see me again. [20]Truly, you will weep and mourn over what is going to happen to me, but the world will rejoice. You will grieve, but your grief will suddenly turn to wonderful joy when you see me again. [21]It will be like a woman experiencing the pains of labour. When her child is born, her anguish

gives place to joy because she has brought a new person into the world. ²²You have sorrow now, but I will see you again; then you will rejoice, and no one can rob you of that joy. ²³At that time you won't need to ask me for anything. The truth is, you can go directly to the Father and ask him, and he will grant your request because you use my name. ²⁴You haven't done this before. Ask, using my name, and you will receive, and you will have abundant joy.

²⁵"I have spoken of these matters in parables, but the time will come when this will not be necessary, and I will tell you plainly all about the Father. ²⁶Then you will ask in my name. I'm not saying I will ask the Father on your behalf, ²⁷for the Father himself loves you dearly because you love me and believe that I came from God. ²⁸Yes, I came from the Father into the world, and I will leave the world and return to the Father."

²⁹Then his disciples said, "At last you are speaking plainly and not in parables. ³⁰Now we understand that you know everything and don't need anyone to tell you anything.* From this we believe that you came from God."

³¹Jesus asked, "Do you finally believe? ³²But the time is coming—in fact, it is already here—when you will be scattered, each one going his own way, leaving me alone. Yet I am not alone because the Father is with me. ³³I have told you all this so that you may have peace in me. Here on earth you will have many trials and sorrows. But take heart, because I have overcome the world."

CHAPTER 17

The Prayer of Jesus

When Jesus had finished saying all these things, he looked up to heaven and said, "Father, the time has come. Glorify your Son so he can give glory back to you. [2] For you have given him authority over everyone in all the earth. He gives eternal life to each one you have given him. [3] And this is the way to have eternal life—to know you, the only true God, and Jesus Christ, the one you sent to earth. [4] I brought glory to you here on earth by doing everything you told me to do. [5] And now, Father, bring me into the glory we shared before the world began.

[6] "I have told these men about you. They were in the world, but then you gave them to me. Actually, they were always yours, and you gave them to me; and they have kept your word. [7] Now they know that everything I have is a gift from you, [8] for I have passed on to them the words you gave me; and they accepted them and know that I came from you, and they believe you sent me.

[9] "My prayer is not for the world, but for those you have given me, because they belong to you. [10] And all of them, since they are mine, belong to you; and you have given them back to me, so they are my glory! [11] Now I am departing from the world; I am leaving them behind and coming to you. Holy Father, keep them and care for them—all those you have given me—so that they will be united just as we are. [12] During my time here, I have kept them safe.* I guarded them so that not one was lost, except the one heading for destruction, as the Scriptures foretold.

¹³"And now I am coming to you. I have told them many things while I was with them so they would be filled with my joy. ¹⁴I have given them your word. And the world hates them because they do not belong to the world, just as I do not. ¹⁵I'm not asking you to take them out of the world, but to keep them safe from the evil one. ¹⁶They are not part of this world any more than I am. ¹⁷Make them pure and holy by teaching them your words of truth. ¹⁸As you sent me into the world, I am sending them into the world. ¹⁹And I give myself entirely to you so they also might be entirely yours.

²⁰"I am praying not only for these disciples but also for all who will ever believe in me because of their testimony. ²¹My prayer for all of them is that they will be one, just as you and I are one, Father—that just as you are in me and I am in you, so they will be in us, and the world will believe you sent me.

²²"I have given them the glory you gave me, so that they may be one, as we are—²³I in them and you in me, all being perfected into one. Then the world will know that you sent me and will understand that you love them as much as you love me. ²⁴Father, I want these whom you've given me to be with me, so they can see my glory. You gave me the glory because you loved me even before the world began!

²⁵"O righteous Father, the world doesn't know you, but I do; and these disciples know you sent me. ²⁶And I have revealed you to them and will keep on revealing you. I will do this so that your love for me may be in them and I in them."

CHAPTER 18

Jesus Is Betrayed and Arrested

After saying these things, Jesus crossed the Kidron Valley with his disciples and entered a grove of olive trees. ²Judas, the betrayer, knew this place, because Jesus had gone there many times with his disciples. ³The leading priests and Pharisees had given Judas a battalion of Roman soldiers and Temple guards to accompany him. Now with blazing torches, lanterns, and weapons, they arrived at the olive grove.

⁴Jesus fully realized all that was going to happen to him. Stepping forward to meet them, he asked, "Whom are you looking for?"

⁵"Jesus of Nazareth," they replied.

"I am he,"* Jesus said. Judas was standing there with them when Jesus identified himself. ⁶And as he said, "I am he," they all fell backwards to the ground! ⁷Once more he asked them, "Whom are you searching for?"

And again they replied, "Jesus of Nazareth."

⁸"I told you that I am he," Jesus said. "And since I am the one you want, let these others go." ⁹He did this to fulfil his own statement: "I have not lost a single one of those you gave me."*

¹⁰Then Simon Peter drew a sword and slashed off the right ear of Malchus, the high priest's servant. ¹¹But Jesus said to Peter, "Put your sword back into its sheath. Shall I not drink from the cup the Father has given me?"

Annas Questions Jesus

[12] So the soldiers, their commanding officer, and the Temple guards arrested Jesus and tied him up. [13] First they took him to Annas, the father-in-law of Caiaphas, the high priest that year. [14] Caiaphas was the one who had told the other Jewish leaders, "Better that one should die for all."

Peter's First Denial

[15] Simon Peter followed along behind, as did another of the disciples. That other disciple was acquainted with the high priest, so he was allowed to enter the courtyard with Jesus. [16] Peter stood outside the gate. Then the other disciple spoke to the woman watching at the gate, and she let Peter in. [17] The woman asked Peter, "Aren't you one of Jesus' disciples?"

"No," he said, "I am not."

[18] The guards and the household servants were standing around a charcoal fire they had made because it was cold. And Peter stood there with them, warming himself.

The High Priest Questions Jesus

[19] Inside, the high priest began asking Jesus about his followers and what he had been teaching them. [20] Jesus replied, "What I teach is widely known, because I have preached regularly in the synagogues and the Temple. I have been heard by people* everywhere, and I teach nothing in private that I have not said in public. [21] Why are you asking me this question? Ask those who heard me. They know what I said."

[22] One of the Temple guards standing there struck Jesus on the face. "Is that the way to answer the high priest?" he demanded.

[23] Jesus replied, "If I said anything wrong, you must give evidence for it. Should you hit a man for telling the truth?"

[24] Then Annas bound Jesus and sent him to Caiaphas, the high priest.

Peter's Second and Third Denials

[25] Meanwhile, as Simon Peter was standing by the fire, they asked him again, "Aren't you one of his disciples?"

"I am not," he said.

[26] But one of the household servants of the high priest, a relative of the man whose ear Peter had cut off, asked, "Didn't I see you out there in the olive grove with Jesus?" [27] Again Peter denied it. And immediately a cock crowed.

Jesus' Trial before Pilate

[28] Jesus' trial before Caiaphas ended in the early hours of the morning. Then he was taken to the headquarters of the Roman governor. His accusers didn't go in themselves because it would defile them, and they wouldn't be allowed to celebrate the Passover feast. [29] So Pilate, the governor, went out to them and asked, "What is your charge against this man?"

[30] "We wouldn't have handed him over to you if he weren't a criminal!" they retorted.

[31] "Then take him away and judge him by your own laws," Pilate told them.

"Only the Romans are permitted to execute someone," the Jewish leaders replied. ³²This fulfilled Jesus' prediction about the way he would die.*

³³Then Pilate went back inside and called for Jesus to be brought to him. "Are you the King of the Jews?" he asked him.

³⁴Jesus replied, "Is this your own question, or did others tell you about me?"

³⁵"Am I a Jew?" Pilate asked. "Your own people and their leading priests brought you here. Why? What have you done?"

³⁶Then Jesus answered, "I am not an earthly king. If I were, my followers would have fought when I was arrested by the Jewish leaders. But my Kingdom is not of this world."

³⁷Pilate replied, "You are a king then?"

"You say that I am a king, and you are right," Jesus said. "I was born for that purpose. And I came to bring truth to the world. All who love the truth recognize that what I say is true."

³⁸"What is truth?" Pilate asked. Then he went out again to the people and told them, "He is not guilty of any crime. ³⁹But you have a custom of asking me to release someone from prison each year at Passover. So if you want me to, I'll release the King of the Jews."

⁴⁰But they shouted back, "No! Not this man, but Barabbas!" (Barabbas was a criminal.)

CHAPTER 19

Jesus Sentenced to Death

Then Pilate had Jesus flogged with a lead-tipped whip.
²The soldiers made a crown of long, sharp thorns and put it on his head, and they put a royal purple robe on him. ³"Hail! King of the Jews!" they mocked, and they hit him with their fists.

⁴Pilate went outside again and said to the people, "I am going to bring him out to you now, but understand clearly that I find him not guilty." ⁵Then Jesus came out wearing the crown of thorns and the purple robe. And Pilate said, "Here is the man!"

⁶When they saw him, the leading priests and Temple guards began shouting, "Crucify! Crucify!"

"You crucify him," Pilate said. "I find him not guilty."

⁷The Jewish leaders replied, "By our laws he ought to die because he called himself the Son of God."

⁸When Pilate heard this, he was more frightened than ever. ⁹He took Jesus back into the headquarters again and asked him, "Where are you from?" But Jesus gave no answer. ¹⁰"You won't talk to me?" Pilate demanded. "Don't you realize that I have the power to release you or to crucify you?"

¹¹Then Jesus said, "You would have no power over me at all unless it were given to you from above. So the one who brought me to you has the greater sin."

¹²Then Pilate tried to release him, but the Jewish leaders told him, "If you release this man, you are not a friend of Caesar. Anyone who declares himself a king is a rebel against Caesar."

¹³When they said this, Pilate brought Jesus out to them again. Then Pilate sat down on the judgement seat on the platform that is called the Stone Pavement (in Hebrew, *Gabbatha*). ¹⁴It was now about noon of the day of preparation for the Passover. And Pilate said to the people,* "Here is your king!"

¹⁵"Away with him," they yelled. "Away with him—crucify him!"

"What? Crucify your king?" Pilate asked.

"We have no king but Caesar," the leading priests shouted back.

¹⁶Then Pilate gave Jesus to them to be crucified.

The Crucifixion

So they took Jesus and led him away. ¹⁷Carrying the cross by himself, Jesus went to the place called Skull Hill (in Hebrew, *Golgotha*). ¹⁸There they crucified him. There were two others crucified with him, one on either side, with Jesus between them. ¹⁹And Pilate posted a sign over him that read, "Jesus of Nazareth, the King of the Jews." ²⁰The place where Jesus was crucified was near the city; and the sign was written in Hebrew, Latin, and Greek, so that many people could read it.

²¹Then the leading priests said to Pilate, "Change it from 'The King of the Jews' to 'He said, I am King of the Jews.'"

²²Pilate replied, "What I have written, I have written. It stays exactly as it is."

²³When the soldiers had crucified Jesus, they divided his clothes among the four of them. They also took his robe, but it was seamless, woven in one piece from the top. ²⁴So they said, "Let's not tear it but throw dice*ª to see

who gets it." This fulfilled the Scripture that says, "They divided my clothes among themselves and threw dice for my robe."*b So that is what they did.

²⁵ Standing near the cross were Jesus' mother, and his mother's sister, Mary (the wife of Clopas), and Mary Magdalene. ²⁶ When Jesus saw his mother standing there beside the disciple he loved, he said to her, "Woman, he is your son." ²⁷ And he said to this disciple, "She is your mother." And from then on this disciple took her into his home.

The Death of Jesus

²⁸ Jesus knew that everything was now finished, and to fulfil the Scriptures he said, "I am thirsty."* ²⁹ A jar of sour wine was sitting there, so they soaked a sponge in it, put it on a hyssop branch, and held it up to his lips. ³⁰ When Jesus had tasted it, he said, "It is finished!" Then he bowed his head and gave up his spirit.

³¹ The Jewish leaders didn't want the victims hanging there the next day, which was the Sabbath (and a very special Sabbath at that, because it was the Passover), so they asked Pilate to hasten their deaths by ordering that their legs be broken. Then their bodies could be taken down. ³² So the soldiers came and broke the legs of the two men crucified with Jesus. ³³ But when they came to Jesus, they saw that he was dead already, so they didn't break his legs. ³⁴ One of the soldiers, however, pierced his side with a spear, and blood and water flowed out. ³⁵ This report is from an eyewitness giving an accurate account; it is presented so that you also can believe. ³⁶ These things happened in fulfilment of the Scriptures that say, "Not

one of his bones will be broken,"* ³⁷ and "They will look on him whom they pierced."*

The Burial of Jesus

³⁸ Afterwards Joseph of Arimathea, who had been a secret disciple of Jesus (because he feared the Jewish leaders), asked Pilate for permission to take Jesus' body down. When Pilate gave him permission, he came and took the body away. ³⁹ Nicodemus, the man who had come to Jesus at night, also came, bringing about thirty-three kilograms* of embalming ointment made from myrrh and aloes. ⁴⁰ Together they wrapped Jesus' body in a long linen cloth with the spices, as is the Jewish custom of burial. ⁴¹ The place of crucifixion was near a garden, where there was a new tomb, never used before. ⁴² And so, because it was the day of preparation before the Passover and since the tomb was close at hand, they laid Jesus there.

CHAPTER 20

The Resurrection

Early on Sunday morning,* while it was still dark, Mary Magdalene came to the tomb and found that the stone had been rolled away from the entrance. ² She ran and found Simon Peter and the other disciple, the one whom Jesus loved. She said, "They have taken the Lord's body out of the tomb, and I don't know where they have put him!"

³ Peter and the other disciple ran to the tomb to see. ⁴ The other disciple outran Peter and got there first. ⁵ He

stooped and looked in and saw the linen cloth lying there, but he didn't go in. ⁶Then Simon Peter arrived and went inside. He also noticed the linen wrappings lying there, ⁷while the cloth that had covered Jesus' head was folded up and lying to the side. ⁸Then the other disciple also went in, and he saw and believed—⁹for until then they hadn't realized that the Scriptures said he would rise from the dead. ¹⁰Then they went home.

Jesus Appears to Mary Magdalene

¹¹Mary was standing outside the tomb crying, and as she wept, she stooped and looked in. ¹²She saw two white-robed angels sitting at the head and foot of the place where the body of Jesus had been lying. ¹³"Why are you crying?" the angels asked her.

"Because they have taken away my Lord," she replied, "and I don't know where they have put him."

¹⁴She glanced over her shoulder and saw someone standing behind her. It was Jesus, but she didn't recognize him. ¹⁵"Why are you crying?" Jesus asked her. "Who are you looking for?"

She thought he was the gardener. "Sir," she said, "if you have taken him away, tell me where you have put him, and I will go and get him."

¹⁶"Mary!" Jesus said.

She turned towards him and exclaimed, "Teacher!"*

¹⁷"Don't cling to me," Jesus said, "for I haven't yet ascended to the Father. But go and find my brothers and tell them that I am ascending to my Father and your Father, my God and your God."

¹⁸Mary Magdalene found the disciples and told them, "I have seen the Lord!" Then she gave them his message.

Jesus Appears to His Disciples

¹⁹ That evening, on the first day of the week, the disciples were meeting behind locked doors because they were afraid of the Jewish leaders. Suddenly, Jesus was standing there among them! "Peace be with you," he said. ²⁰ As he spoke, he held out his hands for them to see, and he showed them his side. They were filled with joy when they saw their Lord! ²¹ He spoke to them again and said, "Peace be with you. As the Father has sent me, so I send you." ²² Then he breathed on them and said to them, "Receive the Holy Spirit. ²³ If you forgive anyone's sins, they are forgiven. If you refuse to forgive them, they are unforgiven."

Jesus Appears to Thomas

²⁴ One of the disciples, Thomas (nicknamed the Twin*), was not with the others when Jesus came. ²⁵ They told him, "We have seen the Lord!" But he replied, "I won't believe it unless I see the nail wounds in his hands, put my fingers into them, and place my hand into the wound in his side."

²⁶ Eight days later the disciples were together again, and this time Thomas was with them. The doors were locked; but suddenly, as before, Jesus was standing among them. He said, "Peace be with you." ²⁷ Then he said to Thomas, "Put your finger here and see my hands. Put your hand into the wound in my side. Don't be faithless any longer. Believe!"

²⁸ "My Lord and my God!" Thomas exclaimed.

²⁹ Then Jesus told him, "You believe because you have seen me. Blessed are those who haven't seen me and believe anyway."

Purpose of the Book

[30] Jesus' disciples saw him do many other miraculous signs besides the ones recorded in this book. [31] But these are written so that you may believe* that Jesus is the Messiah, the Son of God, and that by believing in him you will have life.

CHAPTER 21

Jesus Appears to Seven Disciples

Later Jesus appeared again to the disciples beside the Sea of Galilee.* This is how it happened. [2] Several of the disciples were there—Simon Peter, Thomas (nicknamed the Twin*), Nathanael from Cana in Galilee, the sons of Zebedee, and two other disciples.

[3] Simon Peter said, "I'm going fishing."

"We'll come, too," they all said. So they went out in the boat, but they caught nothing all night.

[4] At dawn the disciples saw Jesus standing on the beach, but they couldn't see who he was. [5] He called out, "Friends, have you caught any fish?"

"No," they replied.

[6] Then he said, "Throw out your net on the right-hand side of the boat, and you'll get plenty of fish!" So they did, and they couldn't draw in the net because there were so many fish in it.

[7] Then the disciple whom Jesus loved said to Peter, "It is the Lord!" When Simon Peter heard that it was the Lord, he put on his tunic (for he had stripped for work), jumped into the water, and swam ashore. [8] The others

stayed with the boat and pulled the loaded net to the shore, for they were only about ninety metres* from shore. ⁹When they got there, they saw that a charcoal fire was burning and fish were frying over it, and there was bread.

¹⁰"Bring some of the fish you've just caught," Jesus said. ¹¹So Simon Peter went aboard and dragged the net to the shore. There were 153 large fish, and yet the net hadn't torn.

¹²"Now come and have some breakfast!" Jesus said. And no one dared ask him if he really was the Lord because they were sure of it. ¹³Then Jesus served them the bread and the fish. ¹⁴This was the third time Jesus had appeared to his disciples since he had been raised from the dead.

Jesus Challenges Peter

¹⁵After breakfast Jesus said to Simon Peter, "Simon son of John, do you love me more than these?"

"Yes, Lord," Peter replied, "you know I love you."

"Then feed my lambs," Jesus told him.

¹⁶Jesus repeated the question: "Simon son of John, do you love me?"

"Yes, Lord," Peter said, "you know I love you."

"Then take care of my sheep," Jesus said.

¹⁷Once more he asked him, "Simon son of John, do you love me?"

Peter was grieved that Jesus asked the question a third time. He said, "Lord, you know everything. You know I love you."

Jesus said, "Then feed my sheep. ¹⁸The truth is, when you were young, you were able to do as you liked and go wherever you wanted to. But when you are old, you will stretch out your hands, and others will direct you and take you where you don't want to go." [19] Jesus said this to let him know what kind of death he would die to glorify God. Then Jesus told him, "Follow me."

[20] Peter turned around and saw the disciple Jesus loved following them—the one who had leaned over to Jesus during supper and asked, "Lord, who among us will betray you?" [21] Peter asked Jesus, "What about him, Lord?"

[22] Jesus replied, "If I want him to remain alive until I return, what is that to you? You follow me." [23] So the rumour spread among the community of believers* that that disciple wouldn't die. But that isn't what Jesus said at all. He only said, "If I want him to remain alive until I return, what is that to you?"

Conclusion

[24] This is that disciple who saw these events and recorded them here. And we all know that his account of these things is accurate.

[25] And I suppose that if all the other things Jesus did were written down, the whole world could not contain the books.

Footnotes

Chapter 1

1:14 Greek *grace and truth*; also in 1:17.
1:16 Greek *grace upon grace.*
1:18 Some manuscripts read *his one and only Son.*
1:19 Greek *and Levites.*
1:21 See Deut 18:15, 18; Mal 4:5–6.
1:23 Isa 40:3
1:26 Or *in*; also in 1:31, 33.
1:27 Greek *to untie his sandals.*
1:34 Some manuscripts read *the chosen One of God.*
1:42 The names *Cephas* and *Peter* both mean "rock."
1:51 See Gen 28:10–17, the account of Jacob's ladder.

Chapter 2

2:1 Greek *On the third day*; see 1:35, 43.
2:6 Greek *2 or 3 measures* [20 to 30 gallons].
2:17 Or *"Concern for God's house will be my undoing."* Ps 69:9.

Chapter 3

3:3 Or *born from above*; also in 3:7.
3:5 Or *spirit.* The Greek word for *Spirit* can also be translated *wind*; see 3:8.
3:7 The Greek word for *you* is plural; also in 3:12.
3:13 Some manuscripts add *who lives in heaven.*
3:14 Greek *must be lifted up.*
3:31 Some manuscripts omit *but he has come from heaven.*

Chapter 4

4:1 Some manuscripts read *The Lord.*
4:20 Greek *on this mountain.*
4:26 Greek *"I am, the one speaking to you."*

Chapter 5

5:2 Some manuscripts read *Beth-zatha*; other manuscripts read *Bethsaida.*
5:3 Some manuscripts add *waiting for a certain movement of the water,* ⁴*for an angel of the Lord came from time to time and stirred up the water. And the first person to step down into it afterwards was healed.*

Chapter 6

6:7 Greek *200 denarii*. A denarius was the equivalent of a full day's wage.
6:14 See Deut 18:15, 18.
6:19 Greek *25 or 30 stadia* [4.7 or 5.6 kilometres, or 3 or 3.5 miles].
6:31 Exod 16:4; Ps 78:24.
6:41 Greek *Jewish people;* also in 6:52.
6:45 Isa 54:13

Chapter 7

7:8 Some manuscripts omit *yet.*
7:37–38 Or *"Let anyone who is thirsty come to me and drink.* [38]*For the Scriptures declare that rivers of living water will flow from the heart of those who believe in me."*
7:40 See Deut 18:15, 18.
7:42 See Mic 5:2.

Chapter 8

8:15 Or *judge me by human standards.*
8:17 See Deut 19:15.
8:25 Or *"Why do I speak to you at all?"*
8:31 Greek *Jewish people;* also in 8:48, 52, 57.
8:39 Some manuscripts read *if you are children of Abraham, follow his example.*
8:57 Some manuscripts read *How can you say Abraham has seen you?*
8:58 Or *"Truly, truly, before Abraham was, I am."*

Chapter 9

9:24 Or *Give glory to God, not to Jesus;* Greek reads *Give glory to God.*
9:35 Some manuscripts read *the Son of God.*

Chapter 10

10:19 Greek *Jewish people.*
10:22 Or *the Festival of Dedication.*
10:34 Ps 82:6

Chapter 11

11:2 This incident is recorded in chapter 12.
11:16 Greek *the one who was called Didymus*.
11:18 Greek *was about 15 stadia* [1.7 miles].
11:19 Greek *Jewish people*; also 11:31, 33, 36, 45, 54.
11:25 Some manuscripts do not include *and the life*.
11:47 Greek *the Sanhedrin*.

Chapter 12

12:3 Greek *took 1 litra* [12 ounces].
12:5 Greek *300 denarii*. A denarius was equivalent to a full day's wage.
12:9 Greek *Jewish people*; also in 12:11.
12:13a Greek *Hosanna*, an exclamation of praise that literally means "save now."
12:13b Ps 118:25–26; Zeph 3:15.
12:15a Greek *daughter of Zion*.
12:15b Zech 9:9
12:31 *The prince of this world* is a name for Satan.
12:32 Greek *lifted up from the earth*.
12:38 Isa 53:1
12:40 Isa 6:10

Chapter 13

13:1 Or *He loved his disciples to the very end*.
13:10 Some manuscripts do not include *except for the feet*.
13:18 Ps 41:9
13:23 Greek *was reclining on Jesus' bosom*. The "disciple whom Jesus loved" was probably John.
13:32 Some manuscripts read *And if God is glorified in him [the Son of Man], God will bring*.

Chapter 14

14:7 Some manuscripts read *If you really have known me, you will know who my Father is*.
14:16 Or *Comforter*, or *Encourager*, or *Advocate*. Greek *Paraclete*; also in 14:26.

Chapter 15

15:25 Pss 35:19; 69:4.
15:26 Or *Comforter*, or *Encourager*, or *Advocate*. Greek *Paraclete*.

Chapter 16

16:7 Or *Comforter,* or *Encourager,* or *Advocate.* Greek *Paraclete.*
16:30 Or *don't need that anyone should ask you anything.*

Chapter 17

17:12 Greek *I have kept in your name those whom you have given me.*

Chapter 18

18:5 Greek *I am;* also in 18:6, 8.
18:9 See John 6:39 and 17:12.
18:20 Greek *Jewish people;* also in 18:38.
18:32 See John 12:32–33.

Chapter 19

19:14 Greek *Jewish people;* also in 19:20.
19:24a Greek *cast lots.*
19:24b Ps 22:18
19:28 See Pss 22:15; 69:21.
19:36 Exod 12:46; Num 9:12; Ps 34:20.
19:37 Zech 12:10
19:39 Greek *100 litras* [75 pounds].

Chapter 20

20:1 Greek *On the first day of the week.*
20:16 Greek *and said in Hebrew, "Rabboni," which means "Teacher."*
20:24 Greek *the one who was called Didymus.*
20:31 Some manuscripts read *may continue to believe.*

Chapter 21

21:1 Greek *Sea of Tiberias,* another name for the Sea of Galilee.
21:2 Greek *the one who was called Didymus.*
21:8 Greek *200 cubits* [300 feet].
21:23 Greek *the brothers.*

Notes:

Notes:

Notes: